...If you lived with the INDIANS OF THE NORTHWEST COAST

by Anne Kamma
Illustrated by Pamela Johnson

SCHOLASTIC INC.

New York Toronto London Auckland Sydney
Mexico City New Delhi Hong Kong Buenos Aires

CONTENTS

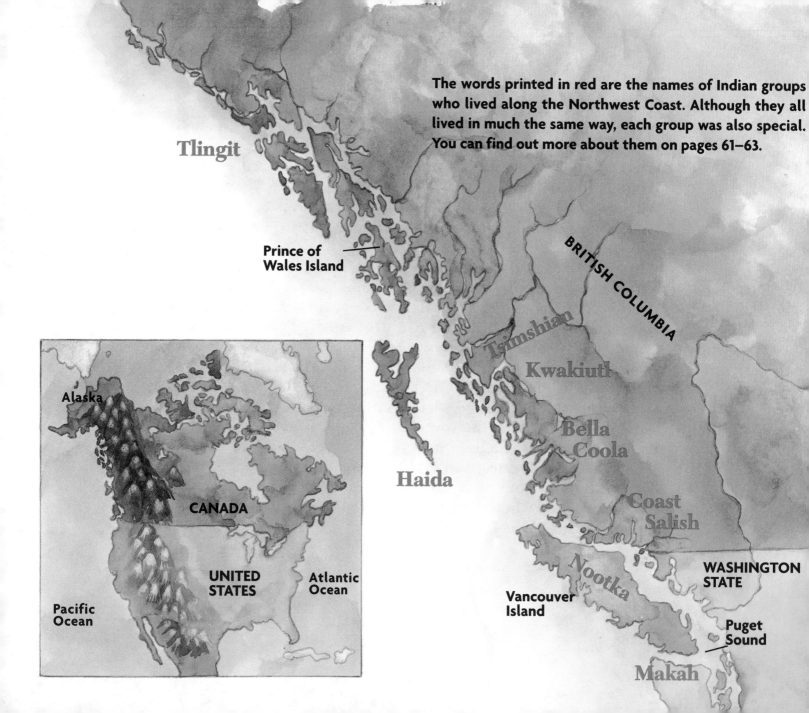

Tlingit

The words printed in red are the names of Indian groups who lived along the Northwest Coast. Although they all lived in much the same way, each group was also special. You can find out more about them on pages 61–63.

Prince of Wales Island

BRITISH COLUMBIA

Tsimshian

Kwakiutl

Bella Coola

Haida

Coast Salish

Alaska

CANADA

UNITED STATES

Atlantic Ocean

Pacific Ocean

WASHINGTON STATE

Nootka

Vancouver Island

Puget Sound

Makah

Introduction

The Indians who lived along the Northwest Coast were quite different from other Indians of North America. If you look at the map, you can see why this was so. A long range of mountains cuts off the coast from the rest of the land. These mountains are so high and so wild, there was almost no place to get across them. So it was very hard for the coastal Indians to get together and share their ideas with Indians living farther east.

But all the coastal Indians were very much alike, even when they lived hundreds of miles apart. That is because they traveled up and down their great "highway," the Pacific Ocean, to visit and trade with one another.

The ocean and the forests gave the people more than they needed. That is why they were the richest of all the Indians living in North America.

This book takes you back hundreds of years to a time before the white settlers arrived. It tells you what it was like to grow up with the Northwest Indians in a village by the sea.

Where would you live?

You would live in a village of wooden houses all lined up facing the beach. Behind you were the dark forest and the mountains.

Some villages had only a few houses, but other villages were so big that they stretched for a mile along the beach.

What was your house like?

Your house was big because there had to be room for many families. It was made of thick boards cut from cedar trees. Some houses were painted with beautiful designs, and some had carved totem poles standing out front. Only the Indians of the Northwest Coast built great wooden houses like these.

The front door wasn't very high, so adults had to bend over to get through it. Sometimes the door was carved through the bottom of the totem pole.

It was dark inside, except for the light from the cooking fires and the smoke hole in the roof. Above you, in the rafters, rows of fish were hung to dry. The walls might be fifteen or twenty feet high — so high that it would take three or four men standing on one another's shoulders to touch the ceiling!

Each family had its own small area to store things and sleep. You'd put all your clothes, tools, and food in wooden boxes and baskets. But you wouldn't need any furniture. The coastal Indians didn't use tables, and the beds and benches were built right into the walls. At night, you'd wrap yourself in a fur blanket and go to sleep on a wooden platform along the wall.

Who lived in your house?

The most important person in your house was the house chief. He and his wife and children lived in the back in an area separated by a beautiful painted screen. Most houses had house chiefs.

All the other families in your house were closely related to the chief. So you would be living not only with your parents, sisters, and brothers, you would be living with your uncles and aunts and cousins and grandparents, too.

The richest families lived close to the chief. If the chief owned slaves, they slept the farthest away from him, near the door.

How would you light your house?

With a lot of little fish!

Every spring, the coastal Indians caught thousands of small, oily fish called eulachon (**yoo**-lah-kon) as they swam from the sea and up the rivers to lay their eggs.

Most of the fish were dried or made into delicious fish oil. But not all the dried fish were eaten. The Indians had discovered that if you put a cedar wick through a dried fish, it burned just like a candle. In fact, these fish came to be known as candlefish.

So your family probably kept a big supply of "candles" to light their living area.

What would you wear?

The weather was mild, so most of the time you wouldn't need many clothes. Women wore skirts made from cedar bark, and men wore breechcloths, or nothing at all. Children wore whatever grown-ups wore. You'd wear a "basket hat" to protect you from the sun.

One thing you would need, though, was rain clothes, because it rained a lot. You would keep dry with a cape or blanket made of woven cedar bark.

Now, you might think that clothes made of bark would be stiff and scratchy, but actually they were soft and warm. That's because the Indians used the soft inner layer of the tree that lies beneath the rough outer bark. The women pounded the inner bark into long, fine fibers.

A basket hat was made from tightly woven cedar roots, so you could wear it in the rain, too.

If you got cold, you'd wrap yourself in your cedar bark blanket or cape. On really cold days, you'd put on your fur robe. Bearskin was popular, but lots of other furs were used, too. Some robes were made from bird skins. The skins from ducks or loons, with all the feathers still attached, were sewn together to make a beautiful warm robe. People almost never wore shoes, even if it was cold or snowy. In fact, some coastal Indians, like the Makah, didn't even have a word for shoes. If it got really, really cold, some might wear deerskin moccasins or wrap woven cedar bark around their feet. If you had to travel in the rugged mountains, though, you would wear moccasins to protect your feet.

Would you ever get dressed up?

Yes. Everyday clothes were not very colorful, but the Indians loved getting dressed up for feasts and ceremonies. You might wear a deerskin tunic, which was painted with beautiful designs, and fancy leggings. Maybe you'd wear a painted basket hat and seashell jewelry, too.

If your father was a chief, he might wear a carved head-dress with fur and sea lion whiskers and a woven blanket like the one the chief in this picture is wearing.

You might also wear a bracelet or necklace made out of sea lion whiskers. Sea lions were usually hunted, but the Indians also had another way of getting whiskers. They stuck some pine branches between the rocks where the sea lions rubbed themselves as they climbed out of the water. The Indians returned later and picked out the whiskers that had been caught in the pine needles.

Why didn't the coastal Indians farm?

Because there was so much food all around them, they didn't need to farm. The rivers were full of salmon every spring, and the sea was full of fish, whales, seals, and shellfish. It was said that there used to be so many salmon, you could walk across the river on their backs.

Fish was as important to the coastal Indians as corn was to other Indians.

What would you eat?

You guessed it — fish! Mostly salmon, but you'd also eat delicious halibut, cod, flounder, candlefish, and herring. Fresh fish was roasted on sticks over the fire. You'd dip it in fish oil and eat it with your fingers.

You'd eat your fish stew with fish oil, too. In fact, just about everything was eaten with fish oil, even desserts. The coastal Indians loved fish oil so much, they put it on their blueberries and strawberries.

Sometimes the hunters brought back deer meat — sometimes the fatty blubber from a whale or seal. Most of the blubber was boiled down into oil. But some was eaten raw at a "blubber feast." You'd wrap a long strip of blubber around your neck, cut off a piece, and swallow it whole. Chewing it was considered very bad manners. It was good manners to keep on eating. The more you ate, the more everyone admired you. Some blubber swallowers ate as many as six strips during the blubber feast.

Would you eat vegetables and bread?

You wouldn't eat vegetables very often, because the coastal Indians didn't farm or have vegetable gardens.

But the women did gather some plants and roots in the forest. In early spring, you'd eat the tender green shoots from cow parsnips and other wild plants. Roasted licorice roots and the sweet-tasting blue camas roots were dug out of the ground with special digging sticks.

The coastal Indians never ate bread because they didn't grow the corn or grain needed to make bread.

Some plants were gathered from the sea. Can you guess what they were?

Answer: seaweed

What was a favorite treat?

Fish eggs. Everyone loved to eat them — cooked, raw, or smoked — just as many people today love caviar, which is also fish eggs.

How was your food cooked?

The coastal Indians did not make pottery. When they needed cooking pots, the men made them out of wood.

So if you wanted to cook some fish stew, you'd use a cooking box made of cedarwood. But you *never* put the cooking box directly over the fire.

This is how it worked: First, you put some water and fish into the cooking box. Then you dropped in some red-hot stones. Pretty soon the stones got the fish stew boiling. To keep it boiling, you kept dropping in more hot stones and taking out the ones that had cooled off.

How would you keep food from spoiling?

Fish rot very quickly, but the coastal Indians knew how to make them last all winter. They dried them.

First, the women cut the fish into thin pieces. Then they hung the pieces up to dry.

But often the weather was too damp for the fish to dry. Then the fish had to be hung in smokehouses, where small fires were kept burning. Smoking is another good way to keep food from rotting. The smoke also makes the fish taste delicious!

Berries were also kept all through the winter. They were either dried or put into containers with fish oil to keep them from rotting.

Clams were dried, too. You could wear them around your neck on a cedar bark string and eat them as snacks.

What were good manners?

It was good manners to pay your debts. It could be embarrassing for a person who didn't. A wood carving that made fun of him might be put up in some public place — on a pole or sometimes on the outside of a house. Then people in the village would laugh at the debtor when they walked past the carving.

It was bad manners to sit wherever you liked. Everyone was seated according to how important they were.

There were special rules for eating. One was: Never show your teeth while you are eating. Another rule was: No matter how thirsty you are, no drinking during the meal! You had to drink your water either before or after you ate. You wouldn't get to eat with your father very often because women and children usually had to wait until the men were finished before they could start eating.

What did girls have to learn?

You'd learn how to handle a canoe. That's how everyone got around, because there weren't any roads. The women of the Northwest Coast were great canoeists. And, of course, you'd learn how to swim.

Mostly you learned to take care of the home, like your mother did. In the summer, women and girls dried and smoked huge quantities of fish and made all the fish oil. They also went on canoe trips to gather berries and shellfish.

Baskets had to be woven so tightly that they could be used for carrying water — you'd learn how to do that, too.

Women wove all the blankets and the cedar bark clothing. A special Chilkat blanket took a woman six months to make, and when it was finished, her father or husband paid her for weaving it. She wouldn't be paid in money, though, because the coastal Indians didn't have money like we do today. Instead, she'd be given something valuable, like a fur robe or shell jewelry.

What was a spirit quest?

When a boy was about twelve, he walked away from his village on a winter day and went deep into the forest.

The boy bathed every day in an icy stream, staying in the water for as long as he could. Then he rubbed himself with branches until his skin bled. He wandered around for days, eating nothing, speaking to no one. At night he waited as the shadows danced by the fire. Why did he do this? He was on a spirit quest to find the powerful spirits who would help him for the rest of his life.

Sometimes the spirits came to him in a dream, sometimes in the form of wild animals. In his dream, the earth might shake and trees might fly through the air. But the boy could not be afraid, for the spirits hated fear. If he was brave, they would tell him what his special talent was going to be — maybe he was going to be a canoe maker, or a seal hunter, or a totem pole carver. Then the spirits would give him magic powers. For without them, no matter how hard he worked, he could never become a success.

After the boy got his magic powers, he went back to his village and told his family what his spirit helpers had said.

What if the spirits didn't come?

Sometimes when a boy was on a spirit quest, he didn't see any spirits. Then he would have to go home and try again another time. It might take him years before he finally found his spirit helpers.

Once in a while, the spirits never came, no matter how many spirit quests a boy went on. Then the boy's family would be ashamed of him, because without special powers, they knew he would never amount to very much.

What did boys have to learn?

All boys learned to be fishermen like their fathers. The Northwest Coast Indians were some of the world's greatest fishermen.

Boys also learned how to cut down a giant cedar tree by setting a small fire at the base of the tree and then chipping away at the burned part. And they learned how to carve masks and make bowls and cooking boxes out of wood.

You'd have to learn how to paddle a sixty-foot canoe through storms and ocean currents, too, so that one day you could go on trading expeditions and war raids.

But you might also have a special talent that you got on your spirit quest. Then your family would find a teacher to help you develop your talent. If your talent was seal hunting, for example, your family would find an expert harpooner. He would teach you how to throw the harpoon. Then one day, after years of hard training, you would finally go on your first seal hunt.

How would you make a canoe?

Only a few men in your village knew how to make a canoe, and they were paid well for their work. If a boy's spirit helper told him that he would be a canoe maker, one of these professional craftsmen would teach him how.

A canoe was made from a cedar log that had been split in half. The coastal Indians didn't have metal tools. Their tools were made of stone, seashells, and wood.

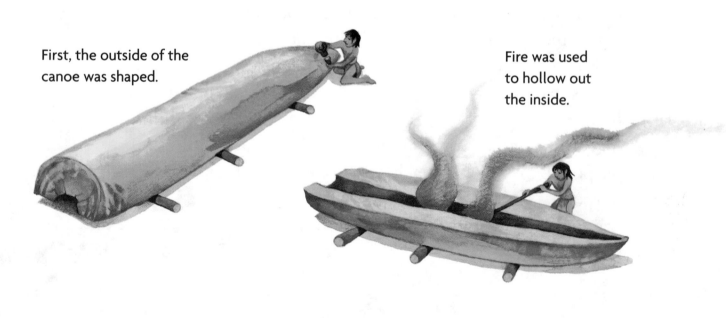

First, the outside of the canoe was shaped.

Fire was used to hollow out the inside.

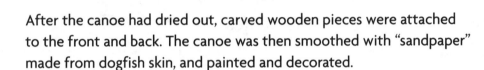

Inside the canoe, water was boiled with hot rocks. When the wood had softened, wooden poles were put in to stretch and widen the sides.

After the canoe had dried out, carved wooden pieces were attached to the front and back. The canoe was then smoothed with "sandpaper" made from dogfish skin, and painted and decorated.

What would you do with an old canoe?

Sometimes children got to paddle it around in shallow water. Sometimes it was used for collecting driftwood along the shore. And sometimes, when there was a big feast, the women cooked food in it!

What happened if you got sick?

The women in your village knew how to make medicines from special plants called herbs. If you got sick, your mother would mix some herbs to make you feel better. Yellow cedar leaves, for example, helped make pain go away. First, your mother chewed the leaves. Then she rubbed them on the place that hurt.

Some of the coastal Indians' medicines are still used today — such as bark of the cherry tree, which was used by the Indians for coughs. Today we use it in cough syrup.

What was a shaman?

A shaman was a medicine man or woman. You asked the shaman to help you with important things — like telling the future, winning wars, and curing the very sick.

The coastal Indians believed that if you got very sick, it was because bad spirits had stolen your soul. It was the shaman's job to travel into the spirit world with a "soul catcher" and bring it back. Otherwise, you would die.

People looked up to shamans. But they were also afraid of them because they controlled such powerful spirits.

How did the coastal Indians believe the world began?

The coastal Indians didn't all agree on how the world began, but their stories were very similar. Here is one story of how it all began:

Long ago the earth was dark and flat. It was full of monsters, but also of the First People, who had magical powers.

The powerful and tricky Raven Spirit lived there, too. The Raven decided to change the earth. He made the mountains and lakes and killed off most of the monsters. But the world was still dark, for there were no sun, moon, and stars in the sky.

Then the Raven heard that some of the First People had all the light in the world stored away in their house.

The Raven decided to steal the light. First, he stole the stars and the moon. Then he stole the sun and threw it into the sky. The light was so powerful, it blasted all the First People off the land and into the sea and the sky.

Without the First People, the land seemed empty, so the Raven created the first humans. But humans were weak, without strong powers. So the Raven asked the First People, who now lived in the sea and the sky, to help the humans. The First People agreed to magically turn themselves into animals, plants, and trees and return to the land so that humans would have plenty of food and wood.

The First People never died, even when the humans killed the animals or cut down the trees. Instead, their spirits returned to their villages in the sea and the sky, where they turned back into the First People again. And as long as humans honored and respected them, the First People would return to help them again and again.

Why did the Indians want the spirits' help?

The coastal Indians believed that everything in the world had a spirit — animals, plants, rocks, even the fog. Most spirits had great magic powers. Human beings needed those strong powers to succeed because their own powers were much too weak.

What was babyland?

Some coastal Indians believed that before babies were born, their souls lived in a place called babyland. Here they played with other baby souls. They even had their own language. Newborn babies talked to one another in this language. But they forgot it as they got older.

Parents did everything they could to make their baby happy. If the baby cried a lot, the parents went to a medicine woman who understood baby language. The woman would try to find out what the baby wanted.

Perhaps it didn't like its name. Perhaps it didn't like to hear its parents arguing. The medicine woman would tell the parents so they could fix the problem.

Why did some coastal Indians have flat foreheads?

Some Indians flattened their babies' heads. They thought that a flat head made you look beautiful.

Among the Coast Salish people, everybody except slaves and the poor did it. Among the Nootka, only important families did it. A baby's bones are soft for the first few months. So it's easy to change their shape before the bones get hard. And it doesn't hurt the baby.

Your mother would flatten your head while you were lying in your cradle. She might put some pads around your head, like the ones in this picture. Slowly the pressure from the pads would change the shape of your head. After some months, when the bones had hardened, your mother removed the pads.

That is the shape your head would have for the rest of your life.

Were grown-ups strict?

Little children were loved and fussed over by everyone in the village. They were never spanked or yelled at.

By age six, you were expected to understand what grown-ups said to you and to mind your elders. You probably wouldn't be bad very often, though, for every child had been told what would happen if you were really bad. The monster Cannibal Woman would carry you off in a big basket and cook you in her cooking box.

Would you go to school?

No, there weren't any places like we have today to go to school. You learned by watching what others did and then trying it yourself. Pretty soon you'd be able to do it, too.

In the winter, storytellers told wonderful stories. They told them again and again. That's how you learned about the history of your family and the great spirits that roamed the earth. Nothing was ever written down, because the coastal Indians didn't have a written language. They used their memories instead!

Why was it important to be rich?

Most North American Indians believed in sharing what they had with others in their village. But the Indians of the Northwest Coast were different. To them, the richer you were, the more you were respected. The richest man in the village became the leader!

Like Europeans, the coastal Indians had nobles, commoners, poor people, and slaves. The richest families controlled the very best fishing places and berry patches — rights passed down from their ancestors who had settled there long ago. If you were rich you also owned big canoes, houses, sea otter robes, goat wool blankets, copper shields, totem poles, and slaves.

The coastal Indians didn't use money the way we do today. But they did sometimes use a kind of shell as money. These long white shells, called dentalia shells, were so rare they were like gold. Indians up and down the coast used them for trading.

Of course, even the poorest families had enough to eat, because there were so many salmon.

What was the most valuable thing you could own?

A copper shield, like the one in this picture. Only the most powerful chiefs had them. Each copper shield was so famous, everyone knew its history and the names of all the chiefs who had owned it before. Copper shields were so valuable that if a poor man found enough nuggets of raw copper to make four shields, he would be rich enough to become a chief!

You also had to be very rich to own a Chilkat blanket. These beautiful blankets were woven by Chilkat women in Alaska. You needed three goat skins to get enough wool for one blanket, and goats were hard to hunt. But the Indians had another way to get goat wool in addition to hunting: During warm weather, when the goats were shedding, the men went high into the mountains and picked the wool off the bushes where the goats had rubbed themselves.

It took a woman six months to weave one of these rare blankets. As she wove, she copied the design her father or husband had painted for her on a wooden panel.

What were wool dogs?

The coastal Indians didn't have sheep, but some of them figured out another way to get wool for their blankets. They raised wool dogs!

These valuable little dogs had thick white wool and were raised by the Salish women around Puget Sound. They were kept in pens on small islands and sheared like sheep. When the family traveled to their fishing grounds, the dogs were brought along. Some families had herds of as many as forty dogs.

There are no wool dogs left today. But an artist named Paul Kane painted one in 1855. This is what the dogs looked like.

Why was the cedar tree important?

The cedar tree was very important to the coastal Indians — almost as important as the salmon. The Indians could make things from cedar that they couldn't make from other kinds of wood that they found in their forests.

The coastal Indians didn't have any saws. But they didn't need them, because cedarwood has a smooth grain, unlike oak or maple. By hammering wooden wedges into the tree trunks, the Indians could split off long, even strips to make boards. All their houses were made of these cedar boards.

And the houses lasted a long time because cedarwood has special oils that keep it from rotting, even when it gets wet. That made cedarwood perfect for houses in a rainy place like the Northwest Coast, and perfect for canoes and cooking boxes as well.

Coastal Indians were great wood-carvers, and the soft cedarwood was easy to carve. They used the wood to make their wonderful masks and totem poles.

The bark of the cedar tree was special, too. When strips of inner bark were pounded with a bark beater, the bark turned into soft, long fibers that could be used for making clothing. Strips of cedar bark were used for baskets, hats, and mats to sit on. Even the long, thin roots found near the surface were pulled out and woven into strong, waterproof baskets.

Prayer to a Cedar Tree

Look at me, friend!
I come to ask you for your dress
Since there is nothing you
cannot be used for.
I come to beg you for this,
Long-Life-Maker.

— Kwakiutl prayer said before pulling bark off cedar trees. The Indians never took so much bark that it killed the tree. They believed that if you killed a tree, the cedar trees nearby would curse you.

Would you go to big parties?

Yes. The coastal Indians loved big parties. That's how they celebrated important events like births, weddings, and building a new house. Some parties lasted ten days. Messengers were sent to other villages with invitations. Guests arrived in canoes and stayed until the party was over. You'd dance and sing and tell stories — and you'd eat, eat, eat! It was good manners to stuff yourself.

These parties were called potlatches, which means "to give away." That's because at the end of the potlatch, the host gave all the guests presents. But everyone didn't get the same present. The more important someone was, the better the present. Powerful chiefs got canoes or fur robes — others just got cedar bark blankets.

You had to be rich to give a big potlatch, and it took families years to prepare. The more gifts you gave away, the more honor you brought to your family. Sometimes the host gave away so many things, he had almost nothing left. Of course, when he was invited to someone else's potlatch, he and his family got valuable presents in return.

Why were potlatches important?

Everyone enjoyed celebrating and having a good time. But potlatches were also important because they gave your family a chance to show people your wealth. The richer your family was, the more other people would honor and respect you.

So potlatches were also a way for everybody to know who was important. A chief might give a potlatch to show that he was still a powerful chief.

Potlatches were also ceremonies that made something official. For example, an old chief who wanted to make his son the new chief needed a potlatch to make it "legal." By attending the potlatch, the guests showed that they accepted his son as the new chief. Even people who hadn't gone to the party now accepted the new chief — the potlatch had made it official.

Why did the coastal Indians carve totem poles?

When white ministers first saw the totem poles, they thought they were religious carvings. But they were wrong. Totem poles were really stories about families. All you had to do was "read" the carvings to learn about the owner's family history.

Totem poles were used for many things. A chief might have a totem pole in front of his house with carvings of his spirit ancestors and of glorious family events. Or the pole might have carvings honoring other chiefs in his family. Sometimes the pole told one story, sometimes many.

You could even include a carving on your totem pole to tell everyone you were sorry about something that had happened and that you had made up with the person you had wronged.

Totem poles were also used to honor dead chiefs. Usually, the coffins sat right on top of the poles. Other totem poles had hollowed-out spaces near the top for the dead chiefs' ashes.

When a totem pole was finished, the owner gave a big pole-raising potlatch and invited hundreds of guests from other villages. Some totem poles were eighty feet high — as tall as a five-story building. Everyone held their breath as the giant pole was pulled upright. One false move and the pole could come tumbling down. If that happened, the host would have to give another, even bigger, potlatch to erase the embarrassment.

Would you get to carve a totem pole?

Totem pole carvers were great artists, respected by everyone. To become one, a boy first spent about ten years studying with a master carver. You learned by watching and then trying it yourself. As you got better, the work got harder. You also learned how to make your own tools out of stone and seashells and wood.

Just as important as learning how to carve was learning how to make the right design for the totem pole. The chief who was having the totem pole made spent hours explaining his family's history. Only when the master carver really understood the history could he start making the design.

When you became a good enough carver, your teacher let you work on his next totem pole. After he drew his design in charcoal, he would draw a line right down the middle of the tree trunk. Everything on his side of the line, he carved. Everything on the other side, you carved, copying exactly what your teacher did.

When you were done carving, it was time to paint. The most popular colors were black, red, blue-green, white, and brown. They were made from natural materials, like ground-up white clamshells mixed with salmon eggs. Some brushes were made with porcupine hairs, others with hairs from your own head. After you pulled out enough hairs to make a little brush, you inserted them into a split stick, trimmed the ends, and started painting!

What was the most important day of the year?

The day the salmon returned in the spring. Everyone was eager to eat fresh salmon again, after months of dried fish. And now you knew there would be food for the coming winter.

Most coastal Indians believed that salmon weren't really fish at all. They were people — some of the First People — who lived in a magic village under the sea. But they turned themselves into salmon to help the Indians.

The very first salmon caught was thought to be a scout sent by the First People. He had come to see if the Indians would treat him with respect. If they didn't, he would tell all the other salmon to stay away.

That's why you weren't allowed to go on fishing right away. Only after prayers were said, and the chief's wife had roasted the first salmon and given everyone a small piece to eat, could you begin fishing again.

A Fisherman's Prayer

Welcome, friend Swimmer,
we have met again in good health.
Welcome, Supernatural One,
you Long-Life-Maker,
for you come to set me right again
as is always done by you.

— from a Kwakiutl prayer greeting the return of the salmon

How would you catch salmon?

The coastal Indians had all kinds of ways, but mostly you used nets, spears, and traps. Those were the fastest ways to catch a lot of salmon — sometimes as many as seven hundred fish in fifteen minutes!

If the river was deep and wide, you'd sweep salmon up with huge nets dragged from canoes.

When the river was shallow, you built fences across the river to trap the fish. Then you could walk on platforms and scoop them up with nets or spear them. When you had caught all the salmon you needed, you took away your fences so the rest of the salmon could get through.

The Life of a Salmon

When salmon are ready to lay their eggs, they leave the sea and swim up-river until they find the place where they were born. Sometimes they have to travel hundreds of miles, leaping over rapids and up waterfalls. But they never turn back, no matter what the dangers. Although many salmon are caught along the way, others survive and swim on.

When they reach the quiet waters of their birthplace, salmon lay their eggs and soon die. After the eggs hatch, young salmon swim down to the sea. There they live as adults for three or four years before they, too, return home to lay their eggs.

Fishing farther upriver was the hardest because the rapids made it impossible to build fences. Then you had to stand on wooden platforms built out over the water and catch salmon with long "dip nets." Sometimes the water was clear enough for you to spear the fish. The coastal Indians were famous for their deadly aim, hitting salmon as they leaped high in the air.

Could you fish anywhere you wanted to?

No. Each family owned the right to fish in certain places. These rights had been in families for hundreds of years. No one else could fish there without permission, and sometimes they would have to pay a fee.

You were lucky if your fishing place was downriver. That's because salmon stop eating once they leave the sea. As they swim upriver, they get thinner and thinner and don't taste as good.

If you lived upriver, you always hoped that those farther down would leave you enough fish. If they didn't, your village might decide to throw some logs in the river to float downriver and break up their traps. Most of the time, though, everyone respected one another's fishing rights. And with so many salmon, everyone usually got their share.

Where would you go in the summer?

Every summer, families packed their belongings into canoes and paddled upriver to their fishing and berry camps. The coastal villages were left empty until the fall.

All summer, your family lived in a shelter covered with cedar bark mats. You might move from place to place several times.

This was the time when you had to work the hardest. Men and boys were busy fishing all day. Women and girls worked nonstop, cutting the fish in pieces and drying and smoking them. There were berries for the women and girls to pick and dry. Even the little children put in long hours.

When the rains started again in the fall, you piled up all the food in your canoe and returned to your village.

Would you fish in the sea, too?

Yes, but mostly you'd stay close to shore, fishing for herring, flounder, and other fish. Some Indians were afraid to go too far out to sea.

But not the Makah, Haida, and Tlingit. They traveled twenty miles out into the ocean in special large canoes to catch halibut. Some halibut weighed two hundred pounds! The fishermen believed that without their spirit helpers, they could never catch these huge and powerful fish.

The fishermen dropped their big wooden hooks to the bottom where the halibut fed. Floats were attached to the other end of the lines. The floats were made of sealskins blown up like balloons. When a float bobbed in the water, the fisherman knew he had a bite and pulled up the halibut. But before he hauled it into the canoe, he clubbed it. Otherwise the struggling fish might overturn his canoe.

For some Indians living farther north where salmon fishing wasn't as good, it was the halibut that gave them plenty of food to eat and dried fish to trade.

Did any coastal Indians go whale hunting?

Many coastal Indians killed whales if they found them stranded in shallow water. But it was the Nootka and Makah who hunted whales on the open seas. Only the chiefs could afford the canoes and equipment needed for such expeditions.

Whale hunting was extremely dangerous, requiring great skill and great spirit power. When a whale was spotted, the canoes rushed toward it. Just as the whale was about to dive, the chief plunged his harpoon deep into its back. Then the other harpooners did the same. The seal-skin floats and lines attached to the harpoon heads made it hard for the whale to dive and get away. Still, it might take all day and night before the whale finally died.

Before they towed the whale to shore, the whalers tied its mouth closed so that it wouldn't fill up with water and sink. Then the whalers headed home, singing songs honoring the whale. They believed that the whale had chosen to help them. And if they honored the whale, it would tell other whales to visit their village, too.

What would you do in the winter?

Winters were stormy and rainy, a time to go to potlatches or to gather around the fire and listen to storytellers. Most exciting of all were the stories acted out by the secret dancing societies. These dances were full of magic tricks — heads might be "cut off" and roll on the floor, or someone might appear to fly through the air. There were also fantastic masks with strings you pulled to show different masks inside.

Each secret society had its own monster spirit. The Kwakiutl had the most famous — the Hamatsa Society with its Cannibal Dancers. Every winter the Cannibal Dancers acted out the story of how Cannibal-at-the-North-End-of-the-World, with his flock of man-eating birds, long ago kidnapped some hunters. After barely escaping with their lives, the hunters returned to their village, taking with them some of the secrets of the Cannibal's great power.

What happened if you became a slave?

If you were caught in a slave raid or captured in war, chances are you would never see your family again. Only if your family was very rich could they afford to buy you back. Even then, most families thought the shame too great to want you back. If they did try to bring you home, they would first have to pay a big ransom. But more important, they would have to hold an expensive potlatch to try to erase the shame your enslavement brought on the family.

Most slaves were women or children who were old enough to work. They lived in the same house as the family who owned them and ate the same food. When a family went to their fishing camp or on trading trips, the slaves came, too. Usually, slaves did the hardest work, like cutting down trees and carrying water. But sometimes they were taught to help their owners build canoes or houses.

When slave boys got older, they might have to paddle their owner's war canoes, and even fight for them when they went on war raids and slave raids.

What did the first European explorers want?

When Captain James Cook, a famous English explorer, sailed up the Northwest Coast in 1777, only a few Europeans had ever been there before. Cook was hoping to find a sea passage across North America, but, like other explorers before him, he found something else — sea otter fur! The rest of the world had never seen such beautiful furs before, so they sold for a great deal of money.

Pretty soon, Americans and Europeans were sailing up and down the Northwest Coast buying furs from the Indians. Everyone was getting rich, but the fur trade helped America in a special way. The War of Independence with England had left the country with little money. Now America could use sea otter fur instead of cash to buy things from other countries.

Did the Indians get rich from the fur trade?

Yes. The Indians were skilled traders, so they knew how to get a good price for each pelt. And they liked the metal tools, wool blankets, and other things that they got in exchange. With better carving tools and paint, they could make their totem poles even bigger and more beautiful.

But being rich also brought problems. Before the fur trade, it might have taken a chief his whole life to save up for one or two potlatches. Now there were potlatches all the time. With so much new wealth, each host tried to outdo the others. Instead of giving the presents away, the hosts sometimes destroyed blankets, canoes, even copper shields, just to show how rich they were.

The fur trade also changed how the coastal Indians worked. Many villages now spent much of their time hunting sea otters and preparing the skins. The Indians also found a way to kill otters more quickly. So many were killed that by 1830 almost all the sea otters were gone.

What happened when the settlers arrived?

The fur traders had wanted to buy as much sea otter fur as possible and then sail back home.

All that changed when lots of people came west to settle. They wanted land to live on — Indian land. Lumber companies and factories for canning fish were built, too. Soon, the coastal Indians had lost most of their land, as well as most of their fishing and hunting grounds.

But worst of all were the new diseases that the settlers brought with them. Smallpox, measles, influenza, and malaria struck one Indian village after another. By 1870, most of the Indians had died. Only one out of five was left alive. Sometimes so many died at one time that there was nobody left in the village to teach the traditions to the children. Surviving Indians lived mostly on small reservations.

Old traditions quickly disappeared. The Canadian government banned potlatches in 1884, and United States missionaries and government officials tried to stop them as well. Wood carving almost died out. By 1890, most Indian families lived in one-family homes, not in large houses with other families.

Today, the coastal Indians live much like other people. But they are also proud of their heritage. Many are hosting potlatches again. Old stories are being told in new, artistic ways. And master carvers, both men and women, are again carving the beautiful totem poles.

INDIAN GROUPS OF THE NORTHWEST COAST

Although all the coastal Indians lived in much the same way, there were some differences from group to group.

The map on page 4 shows where the seven largest Indian groups lived along the Northwest Coast. As you can see, each group was known for something special:

The **Coast Salish (SAY-lish)** lived in British Columbia and around Puget Sound in Washington State. They were famous for their wool dogs (see page 35). They were also great sturgeon fishermen. Sturgeons were the largest fish caught by the coastal Indians. Some are twenty feet long and weigh as much as a small elephant.

The **Nootka (NOOT-ka)** lived on Vancouver Island in British Columbia. They are also called Nuu-chah-nulth, which means "all along the mountains."

The Nootka were famous seamen, warriors, and whale hunters (see page 52). They built beautiful big canoes for traveling the ocean.

The **Makah (mah-KAH)** are related to the Nootka, but they lived on the tip of the Olympic Peninsula in Washington State. The Makah, too, were great canoe makers and whale hunters. We know a lot about the Makah from studying one of their ancient villages, called Ozette. It was buried in a mud slide more than five hundred years ago.

Ozette was discovered in 1970. When the archaeologists cleaned away the mud, they were amazed to find a whole village. Most of the things were still there, just the way they had been on that day long ago when disaster struck.

The **Kwakiutl (KWAH-key-yoo-tel)** lived on the northern part of Vancouver Island and nearby coast of British Columbia. They were great wood-carvers and were also famous for their Cannibal Dancer ceremonies (see page 55). The outside walls of their houses were painted in big, colorful designs.

The **Bella Coola (bel-la COO-la)** lived in British Columbia near the Bella Coola River, where they fished for candlefish (see page 10) and salmon. They were known for their beautiful carved masks. The Bella Coola were great hunters, especially of mountain goats.

The **Haida (HI-duh)** lived on the Queen Charlotte Islands in British Columbia and on Prince of Wales Island in Alaska. They were daring seamen and fierce warriors. They traveled up and down the coast in their magnificent carved canoes — some more than sixty feet long, holding sixty people. The Haida were the first coastal Indians to carve totem poles.

The **Tsimshian (SIM-shan)** lived along the Skeena and Nass rivers in British Columbia. Unlike most coastal Indians, some Tsimshian lived in the mountains along the rivers. The rest lived by the sea. The rivers made it easy for them to travel back and forth to trade with one another.

Like the Haida and Tlingit, the Tsimshian were known for their splendid totem poles. They were also great hunters. In the winter, they wore snowshoes when traveling in the high country.

The **Tlingit (KLING-git)** lived along the southern coast of Alaska. The Tlingit were famous for their beautiful Chilkat blankets, which were woven by a small band of Tlingit called the Chilkat.

The Tlingit were also great traders and businessmen. To get copper, caribou skins, and other valuables, the Tlingit hiked across steep mountains and traded with the Athabascan living on the other side. All the other Indians living along the coast wanted copper and caribou skins, too. So they paid the Tlingit a good price for them. That's how the Tlingit became rich.

For my mother

ACKNOWLEDGMENTS

With grateful thanks to the staff at the Smithsonian National Museum of the American Indian; the staff at the American Museum of Natural History; the staff of the New York Public Library, Bloomingdale Branch; Sue Harris, of the Stark Museum of Art, Orange, TX; Laila Williamson, anthropologist at the American Museum of Natural History; my wonderful editor, Eva Moore; Roberta Burkan, docent at the American Museum of Natural History; and Ellen Levine, for her insightful comments and suggestions. "Prayer to a Cedar Tree" is reprinted from Through Indian Eyes *(The Reader's Digest Association, 1995). "A Fisherman's Prayer" is reprinted from Hilary Stewart's* Indian Fishing *(Seattle: University of Washington Press, 1977).*

ISBN 0-439-26077-9

Art direction by Ursula S. Albano
Book design by Christopher Motil

12 11 10 9 8 7 6 5 4 3 2 1   2 3 4 5 6 7/0

Printed in the U.S.A.
First Scholastic printing, April 2002